Kirti Prasad 'Aarohi'

A Fistful Of Sky

A Collection of Poems

BlueRose ONE .com
Stories Matter

First Published in February 2023

ISBN: 978-93-5741-032-8

BLUEROSE PUBLISHERS

www.BlueRoseONE.com

info@bluerosepublishers.com

+91 8882 898 898

Cover Design:

Aman Sharma

Typographic Design:

Namrata Saini

Distributed by: BlueRose, Amazon, Flipkart

Dedication

A fistful of sky is dedicated to my mother Dr. Jayalakshmi M and my sweetheart, my son Vihaan Bhargava.

Ma's fantastic grip on the language helped me a lot in choosing words.

Thank you Mummy for being the inspiration you always are!

Thanks Vihaan for showing me the way and giving me reasons to smile.

Yours Forever,

Kirti Prasad 'Aarohi'

Contents

Love

Love is an ocean,
Full of grace
Love contains peace,
And acquires pace
Love is a star,
With charm and brilliance
Love is a flower,
With beauty and fragrance
Love inspires,
And illuminates the mind
Love exists forever,
Like sunshine.

- Kirti Prasad 'Aarohi'

(I read this poem on 14th Nov., '96 in school)

Nature

Nature is a spell,
Which makes me crazy.
Nature is something,
Mysterious and breezy.

There's a strange beauty,
In the high mountains with pearly snow
In the monsoon's grey clouds,
And the sevencoloured rainbow.

How comely look,
The Sun’s rays.
How beautiful are the ocean's
Blue guttering waves.

The laughter of the waterfalls,
Seems God's voice
Heart's sadness is removed,
When I hear wind's noise.

It seems I'm in heaven,
When the soft breeze blows.
When pansies bloom,
And the lake slowly flows.

You never can imagine,
Nature's aspects
Nature is lovelier,
Than a man expects.

- **Kirti Prasad 'Aarohi'**

Friend

Friend is a smile,
Full of charm
Friend is sky,
Lovely and calm.
Friend is sacred,
Without any stain.
Friend never gives,
A bit of pain.
Friend is a rose,
Fragrant, beautiful.
Friend is reliable,
Always truthful.

- Kirti Prasad 'Aarohi'

Learning

Learning is something,
More precious than gold.
Learning is never,
Bought or sold.
Learning is the doorway,
To success.
Learning makes the mind,
Perfect and flawless.
Learning can remove,
The sore miseries of life.
Learning accustoms,
The bright aspects of life.

- Kirti Prasad 'Aarohi'

My Umbrella

I was there in a rainy evening,
With an umbrella of mine.
It was flimsy, couldn't shield me.
So I sat under a pine.
It wasn't safe to sit there,
Suddenly I remembered.
I got up from that place,
And saw a flying bird.
It was flying in the air,
And was very swift.
I felt God had given her,
A very beautiful gift.
I had to go home,
So I started walking.
There was no one, but my umbrella,
To whom I was talking.

- Kirti Prasad 'Aarohi'

Mother

Mother, remember me,
When I am not with you.
I can't forget you ever,
'Coz I love you.

I feel your love
When you give me a scold.
Your love can never be,
Bought or sold.

Whenever I succeed,
Your eyes fill with arrogant tears.
When I do something nice,
House echoes with your happy cheers.
I consider you to be greater than God.
I am fortunate that you pull my ears.

You are anguished when I am in despair.
I cannot forget, your affection & care.

You are the person, I adore most.
Your pity & love, are really very rare.

You fulfill, all my needs
When I am in pain, your heart bleeds.
When I am overjoyed, you are glad
A variable life - your heart leads.

I feel very happy
When you wrap me in a blanket in a cold night.

My mind is placated,
When you give me love's soothing light.
I feel very nice in your company.
I feel that you are my eye's sight.

- Kirti Prasad 'Aarohi'

(This poem is dedicated to my Mother who is loving, caring and an unparalleled person.)

My land

She was a land, where elders were respected.
She was a land, where jealously was neglected.
She was a land, of elegant nature's beauty.
She was a land, where no one ignored their duty.
She was a land, where existed peace's abode.
She was a land which was greeted by the Lord.
She was a land, where valiants lived & died.
She was a land whose beauty was difficult to find.
She was a land, where glittered the sunshine.
She was a land, which was bright & fine.
But today, she's covered by a black shroud.
She's crying and weeping just like a rainy cloud.
Today, no one is wiping her tears,
She's gloomy, when every nation is having cheers.
Because her children are constantly deceiving,
Busy in their work & are conceiving,
That they would be wealthy,
By cheating their country.
Let's try, to make 'em understand,
That no one becomes wealthy by cheating their land.

- Kirti Prasad 'Aarohi'

Didi, I Love You!

I can feel the love
That you have for me in your heart.
I pray to God with pure dedication
That we may never depart.

My life has been kindled.
By the warmth of your twinkling eyes.
Your lovely face reminds me
Of pretty butterflies.

Without you, I'm like a boat,
That has lost its rudder.
When I think of being away from you,
I don't do anything but just shudder.

You don't know, how much I love you.
For the sheer warmth of your love sustains me.
Whenever I want to give up the struggle,
Your profound love restrains me.

We'll be with each other forever -
That's the will of fate.
I'll be there to love you and help you,
As you are my life - long mate.

(Written for darling sis, Gunjan Didi)

- Kirti Prasad 'Aarohi'

Date - 17th May, 1998
Day - Sunday
Time - 9:15 A.M.

Dream

I dream of a world
Where blossoms are scattered everywhere.
I dream of a world
Full of deep affection and care.
I dream of a world
Where there are no sorrows and no pains,
Where there is only LOVE
And Love's binding chains.
There'll be a small hut
With gardens all around.
There I'll get a strange peace
That I have never found.

- Kirti Prasad 'Aarohi'

Date - 19th Sep, 1998
Day - Saturday

Smile

What's there in a smile?
Somebody may ask.
Just a sheen of hope,
And the fulfilment of task.

So cast a sunny smile
Whenever you can.
And it will accomplish
Whatever you plan.

Never act miserly
In giving smiles.
For the happiness, it'll create
Will spread on to miles.

What is a smile?
A health tonic,
It is a healer
of the diseases - chronic

It will take away
All the tensions encasing your mind.
It can be noticed
Even by a person who's blind.

Smile is a priceless gift
Given to us by the lord.
Pass it on to everybody
And thereby please God.

Smile loosens gently
All the knots of sorrow.
It will give your pleasure
Soothing and thorough.

So give a broad smile
And brighten up your face.
Gloom from your life,
It will efface.

- Kirti Prasad 'Aarohi'

Date - 4th Aug., 1998
Day - Tuesday
Time - 06:02 P.M.

Memories

Memories are as beautiful
As a delicate pot of roses.
But they create a bitterness
Which agony causes.

We remember those happy moments
And we want to get them back.
But how to tell the heart
That they are packed up in a sack.

A sack which can never be opened
As it's the sack of time.
And time never waits
Waiting for it is a crime.

We pine and pine
Remembering that warmth of love.
But our cry isn't heard
Even by the lord above.

O, Lord please bring back those days.
I want nothing more.
Because the agony of my heart
Hurts me more and more.

I can't bear this pain
And this loneliness.
I just want to get back
Those days of happiness.

- Kirti Prasad 'Aarohi'

The Morning Star

I am your humble servant, O Morning Star!
Accept my love, accept these my regards.

Your mercy is indescribable,
Though tried to described by all the bards.

You shed your blood to purify our sins.
You loved those who pierced your body with pins.

You relaxed the tensed, you healed the diseased.
You believed in God when everybody had ceased.

You never bothered for yourself, but for others
cared.
All their grieves and plains, every time you
shared.

As we try to come close to you, we are troubled
by the Devil.
Oh Lord! therefore help us, to resist the evil.

Our souls are thirsty to drink the nectar of your love.
Our ears are eager to hear your words.
So shower your blessings on everyone,
All the creatures and all the birds.

- Kirti Prasad 'Aarohi'

Burden

There's a sea of emotions
Deep within my heart,
Where feelings are bubbling out,
And a void that, forever, will last.

My heart just shudders
At the thought of being alone.
I know I can't help it
I can only mourn.

The blossoms have drooped
The lake has dried.
How dark is this day!
The light has died.
My only hope is my saviour
Who reigns in the placid heaven
Now life is a burden -
Cumbersome and heavy-laden.

- Kirti Prasad 'Aarohi'

Date - 9th Jan, 1999
Day - Saturday
Time - 1:40 P.M.

An Ordinary Card

A very ordinary card, not even your worth
Is sent to you to tell you, "You're loveliest on the earth."

So, lovely wishes come out, deep from my heart.
May elation and happiness, from you never depart.

May the new year proves to be, the turning point of your life.
And a burning candle, which lights up your life.

May dear God bless you, with all exultation.
All grieves are effaced, and good things in commemoration.

- Kirti Prasad 'Aarohi'

I wrote this poem on the date mentioned above to write it on a New Year card meant for my Didi. This poem is dedicated to her, although, I know it isn't even her worth. However hard I'll try, I'll never be able to repay the debt which I owe to her. So this poem is not meant for repaying the debt but for expressing the love which resides in my heart for her.

Sibling Love

I see the quivering stars
And I remember you.
I see title girls walking along the knolls
And I remember you.

I see the green leaves
Brightly shining with the
Light of Sun.
And I remember you.

I see the fragrant beautiful
Blossoms blooming
And I remember you.

I see the haze of clouds
Stealthily misting the Azure sky.
And I remember you.

"You appear to be a rose
fresh and sweet"
Keeps on saying my heartbeat.

You are a princess, not the one
With silky, flamboyant robes
And ornaments studded with

Previous gems, but you are
The one with a golden heart
And the eternal beauty of the soul.

You cherished me when I wasn't
Able to look after myself.
You were always there, whenever
I encountered difficulties.

When I realise that we are
Far away from each other,
My heart droops, I become lifeless.
The very thought petrifies me.
May you thrive, even in adverse circumstances.
May the tree of life.
Be laden with the perfumed flowers of happiness.
And may the love of God
Be constantly showered on you.

- Kirti Prasad 'Aarohi'

A simple poem - creation of love for my elder sis, Gunjan.

15th April, 1999
Sunday
1.15 p.m.

Love is what?

Love is what?
Perhaps the rippling sheen on a still lake.
It is not a one-way traffic.
It's not a pact of give and take.

Love is profound, love is deep.
Love is a treasure, forever to keep.
Love is peace, love is blind
Love is a pearl on a silken heap.

Love is sacrifice, love is forgiving.
Love is losing and not retrieving.

Love is life, love is all
It's not distrust but is believing.

- Kirti Prasad 'Aarohi'

Time 10:20 pm
March, 1999

Success

Goals are what we decide.
But they are not easy to achieve.

You've got to do two things for that -
Work hard and believe

That however difficult the path may be
You are prepared to walk
And, automatically, you get the key to Success.
Now, all you have to do
Is to open the lock.

But that requires firm determination
And sacrifice of desires.
These are some of the virtues.
Which everybody admires.

But do remember,
Failure is not all end
It simply implies - some of your ways
You have to mend.

Success is your dream.
It can come true
If only you trust yourself.
And never be blue.

- Kirti Prasad 'Aarohi'

16th April, 1999
11:40 am

Oh! How I Wish!

How I wish to be a painter!
Painting all the lovely creatures.
Shaping all the memories of life.
Giving beauty to natural features.

Painting mountains, painting birds,
Painting rivers and painting flowers;
What peace I would get
Painting thoughts in lonely hours!

What beautiful emotions would be there
In that beautiful potpourri of hues.
I'll divulge all the secrets of nature
And all the life's mysterious clues.

Sitting with an easel,
And many brushes;
Painting Life and
A girl who blushes
Life won't be monotonous;
It would be so lovely,
Painting all the memories golden

And the sun's beams - soothing and comely.

My feelings would come down on my paintings.
My hands would be bound by beauty's clutch.
Gratification will stroke me constantly
With it's mellow and silken touch.

Painting all the silvery thoughts,
The sheen of moon and the smile of day.
I know my dream will surely come true
For "Where there's a Will there is a Way".

- Kirti Prasad 'Aarohi'

This poem was written by me when my English teacher,Ms. Shroti, asked the class to write a short stanza about someone's work we would like to do after teaching a Rabindranath poem, 'I wish I were.'

16th April, 1999
11:40 am

Life is Helter Skelter

I am an untended weed,
Cared for by none
Moon doesn't shine in my life,
Gloomy is the sun.

Breeze doesn't sway,
And stars never shine,
When will it end?
For how long will I pine?

O, what a lonely life!
And how ignored I feel!
I'll stay sick forever.
My wounds will never heal.

Don't shun me, O Lord!
As I seek your shelter.
I'm completely in despair;
Life is helter skelter.

Forgive me, O Lord!
For I've hurt you so much.
Now I don't want to stay away,
I want to be in your clutch.

- **Kirti Prasad 'Aarohi'**

18th April, 1999
Sunday
10 to 7 am

Waves

These undulating oceans,
How they play with the waves!
And in what a playful manner,
Every wave behaves!

How beautiful is their world!
And how suave their work!
Their beauty is an enchanting web,
Which nobody can shirk.

These beautiful blue blankets,
Will placate all troubles.
Being with them
Sorrow vanishes and happiness doubles.

I want to have them inside me;
I want to feel that peace.
O waves! Come and dwell in me;
Listen to me, please!

- Kirti Prasad 'Aarohi'

5.06 pm
31st May, 1999
Monday.

The Pleading of a Young Girl

Let me not be drawn in the sweeping seas,
For they just look beautiful,
But they harbour a ferment of death.
Don't kill me at such a tender age,
For I've seen very little of the world.
Let me take a little breath.

Don’t let me be stung by little bees,
For they just look colourful,
But within their sting is lingering pain.
Don't mutilate all my desires,
For there's shining hope in my heart
of playing heartily with the lovely rain.

Let me not fly in the high skies,
For they just look serene,
But they cause precarious falls
Don't entangle me in the web of death,
For I want to smell the rain-soaked soils.
And admire trees graceful and tall.

Let me not be lost in the strong winds
For they not only look violent
But also deep inside harbour inevitable ruin.
O, let me thrive, let me thrive a little.
Don't break my heart so ruthlessly
For it is innocent and genuine.

Kirti Prasad 'Aarohi

4:45 p.m.
Saturday
16th Oct, 1999

Faltering Strides

Faltering strides, wavering thoughts,
Misled, meandered from the path,
I happened to be one of the victims,
Who had to leave their homes and hearth.

No bright sunshine, all dusk is life
Like idle iron, all rust is life.
Not a single drop of love;
It's dry, too dry, you have to chew it hard,
A dry risk is life.

My heart aches, my soul bleeds,
I asphyxiate in the dark lanes.
Happy life has to be led,
Not by heart, but by brains.

Who can give you a warm smile?
Who can provide you with a bundle of joy?
Who cares for your feelings and for your emotions
World treats your heart just like a toy.

- Kirti Prasad 'Aarohi'

15th Aug, 2000
Tuesday
Around 1 p.m.

Wicks of candles

Wicks of candles
Burn and burn,
Blanketing the air with greasy smoke,
And soon putting on flamboyant robes,
Heavy robes sliding over the candle
And then on the wooden table,
The flame, the fiery flame, the
Luminous flame, the heart of light, the centre of everything.
The zestful flame, perhaps a little morose too;
Disseminating an unknown message;
Is it a shroud or a shred of joy?
Does it strengthen or does it destroy,
The forlorn hope lurking somewhere,
The innate talent or natural flair?
It burns and burns
With an untold dejection, or perhaps
With bursting elation.
May it be joy, may it be sorrow,
The wick burns
And also churns the air,
Spreads also the much sought-after light

May it be dim or dull or profuse or bright.
It burns and it dies
Into an amorphous mass
To take birth again,
To get resurrected.

- Kirti Prasad 'Aarohi'

(Wrote for a Christian magazine. This poem wasn't selected)

6:15 pm
Sunday
15/7/2001

I Was Asked

I was asked to write a poem.
I kept searching for words
Till I saw you,
And then words flew from my pen like birds
And became immortal on the pages of my diary.

I was asked to sing a song.
I kept searching for notes
Till I saw you,
And then notes themselves got strung into a
beautiful garland
And became the voice of my soul.

I was asked to create a picture.
I kept searching for hues
Till I saw you,
And then the blush of your cheeks tinted my
canvas.
And made it the image of God forever to cherish.

I was asked to heal my bruised soul.
I kept searching for balms.
Till I saw you
And then the pain melted,
Wounds vanished and I became
The healthiest one on earth.

I was asked to cast a smile.
I kept searching for reasons
Till I saw you,
And then the smile bud blossomed on my face
I Laughed for no reason at all.

I Was asked to praise beauty.
I kept searching for paeans
Till I saw you,
And then paeans became my speech
And I felt beauty in the ugliest aspect of life.

Kirti Prasad 'Aarohi'

This poem was selected in an anthology "Poetry of the Blooming Buds" published by the Poetry Society of India way back in 2001 when I was a Class XI student.

1 : 15 pm
Friday
24th Aug., 2001

"A bit and I am Almost There"

Aspirations, ambitions, dreams
Blossom and life beams.
The cream of life they are,
But peace and rest they mar.

The glowing stars of distant,
Look pretty, but you're hesitant
To walk on and pick a few
Alone, without the crew.

High up in the sky they glitter and tempt,
The feeble mind, fearing contempt,
The mind that fears the laws of world,
Has a will that's slightly curled,

That wants to relish the thrill of laurels
Still wants to rest in comfort floral.
Who deserves the Pearl tell me,
An escapist or a diver's plea?

Length of the errand, worries it the most.
Broods impending hardships, standing on the
coast.

O Feeble mind! leave this cave
Not fake, but true troubles you bear.
And all along the journey say,
"A bit and I am almost there."

- Kirti Prasad 'Aarohi'

11 : 45 am
Thursday
20th Sept., 2001

Poetry

The waves of heart, the image of life,
Poetry is a sacred web.
Life's crescendo and stagnation.
And what else can be it's ebb?

Effortlessly it does express
The words unsaid and deeds undone.
The only weapon of the light lipped
When his emotions swiftly run.

A mere motion of the fingers
And the flow of ink cheap
Adds on to it a jewel new
Bright and brilliant forever to keep.

An epistle written to oneself.
It is the golden voice of soul.
But who honours the complex creature
In this very cosmos whole.

Misery pool of innocent eye,
Shout of mirth and elation pearled,
One which stands for romance and beauty
Poetry is that flag unfurled.

- Kirti Prasad 'Aarohi'

12 : 40 pm
4th Sept., 2001
Tuesday

Before life ends

Engrave your name on every stone
With the greenness of emeralds.
Make a mark on earthly sands,
Hurry! Before this life melts.

Spread like musk, bloom like rose.
Be talked about far and wide.
It mustn't be that no one knows
When thee came and when died.

Let the firmament sing your praises.
And the earth swell up with pride.
Do the undone say the unsaid,
And walk off complacent eyed.

You'll be scorned by many a man
Neglect all that, stick to your plan.
You will relish the cool of snow
Only when your body tans.

Talent is like an amorphous gem
Dusty, musty and sans shine.
Worry not if you lack
'Coz labour will produce nine.

Gems, well cut & shiny
Prettier and devoid of dust!
Such is the power of labour, Dear!
Labour alone is worth your trust.

Life's short, too short to live.
You can still be immortal if
Less you take from this world
And to it more you give.

- Kirti Prasad 'Aarohi'

Tears and Dreams

If eyes harbour tears,
They also harbour dreams.
While one makes us cry
The others make us beam.

If tears are believed,
Why dreams are suspected?
While one is welcomed
The other rejected?

Calibre cannot change them
But they enrich caliber.
While tears gift sorrow.
It's joy that Dreams deliver.

Let's welcome dreams now.
Let's allow them to us gladden.
'afore tears win the battle
'afore they us sadden .

- Kirti Prasad 'Aarohi'

August 28, 18
Agra

Loyal as ever,
Forgetful of Mistakes & Pain
Crazy me, Stupid too
Have in Love again!

- Kirti Prasad 'Aarohi'

August 28, 2018
Agra

He Could Have

He could've said,
He should've said.
He left the journey
And the map unread.
Was it all a Lie?
Not a hint of truth?
No breeze serene,
Just wind uncouth?

- Kirti Prasad 'Aarohi'

Just A QUERY

Is there power in somebody's curse?
Heartfelt curse, precise & terse?
Helpless with just a penny in purse
But strength to move on
With broken dreams to nurse.

- Kirti Prasad 'Aarohi'